My Life Manager©

Katrina Mulberry

Published by Manage Me, LMS

(Life Management Systems), Inc.

www.ManageMe.ca

My Life Manager App launched 2021

Library and Archives Canada Cataloguing in Publication.

Mulberry, Katrina

My Life Manager: A Personalized Record-keeper Belonging to:_____

ISBN 978-0-9869543-0-6

1.Self-publishing. I. My Life Manager

Manage Me™

Welcome to My Life Manager©.

Are you organized? Anyone **can** be, but how often do you find yourself wasting precious time searching for an important document. It pays to be organized and to know where your important files and documents are when you need them.

Whether it's your net worth, current debt, life insurance policy values, SIN, Service card or passport number, you now have a safe and simple way to keep all your information organized and in one place. Keep your Financials current and know your cost of living by completing the included budget sections.

My Life Manager by Manage Me , LMS (Life Management Systems) is a tool to fill with records of importance and personal information that will help one become better organized and prepared for everyday events. Whether its making a budget, applying for a bank loan, setting a goal, or wondering where to keep important receipts, reminders, warranties, resumes, school transcripts and job applications, Rental Agreements My Life Manager© has a place for it all.

- o Personal Information
- o Contacts
- o Goals
- o Calendar for Reminders
- o Financial Snapshot
- o Budget
- o Assets
- o Insurance
- o Debts
- o Estate Planning
- o Wallet
- o Personal Other

ISBN978-0-9869543-0-6

0 617737 254844

Manage Me ™

DISCLAIMER

IT IS RECOMMENDED TO USE PLASTIC PROTECTOR SHEETS TO KEEP ORIGINAL DOCUMENTS IN EACH CHAPTER AFTER THE NOTES SECTION.

Manage Me™

CONTENTS

Manage Me™

Personal Information

Include originals via PDF or pic file to support chart"

IN CASE OF EMERGENCY:

Personal Health Number: _____

My full legal name & address _____

Next of Kin & contact number _____

Whom to notify & contact number _____

Date Of Birth_____   Blood Type : _____

Allergies_____

Current Dr & contact number_____

Current Meds _____

_____

Medical Diagnoses_____

_____

_____

Organ Donor_____ Living Will _____

Immunizations: _____

_____

Most Recent medical procedure _____

_____

_____

Manage Me™

Personal Information

Document	Name	Date of Expiry	Number	Other
Birth Certificate				
Gov ID				
Drivers License				
Passport				
Medical Care Card				
Marriage Cert.				

Document	Name	Date of Expiry	Number	Other

Notes:

Attach a recent photo of yourself

Contacts

Complete the following chart with emergency, personal, medical, business and other contacts' information.

Contacts

Name	Relationship	Email	Mobile	Address	Country
Emergency Contacts					
Personal Contacts					
Medical Contacts					

Name	Relationship	Email	Mobile	Address	Country
Business Contacts					
Other Contacts					

Notes:

Goals

List your life, work and family goals.

Life Managemervices ™

Goals

Goals	Description (Upload Pictures)	Priority	Set Date	Goal Date	Achieved Date
Life					

Goals	Description	Priority	Set Date	Goal Date	Achieved Date
Work					
Family					

Notes:

Annual Calendar
for reminders

Calendar for annual reminders

For example:

January	February	March	April	May	June
Annual Budget review	Car insurance due 15th	Spring break	Income Tax 30th		Home Insurance
Goals	RRSP contributions	Plant grass seeds	Mortgage anniversary	Register summer activities	Mother's BD
Claimed ___ (Check off when received)	RESP___	Change Oil in red car		Annual health check	
Get Teeth Cleaned					

July	August	September	October	November	December
Property taxes	Clean eaves	Clean Furnace and ducts	Winterize home		Anniversary
		Personal Insurance premiums due	Winterize car (snow tires)		
		Change oil in red car			Change oil in red car

January	February	March	April	May	June

July	August	September	October	November	December

Financial Snapshot

It is recommended to complete the Budget, Assets and Debts Sections prior to this Financial Snapshot.

Manage Me™

Financial Snapshot

Account	Account Number	Financial Institution	$ Opening Balance	$ Current Value
Assets			$	$
Bank:				
Cash & term accounts				
Investments:			$	$
Real Estate				
Investment Portfolio Value				
Stocks Bonds Mutual Funds				
Retirement Funds				
RESPS				
Life Insurance				
Personal Items (Art, jewelry,)				

Account	Account Number	Financial Institution	$ Opening Balance	$ Current Value
Home items (Of value)				
Vehicles				
Recreational items:				
Other Assets:				
Debts:				
Credit Cards				
Mortgage				
Loans				
Other Debts				
TOTAL ASSETS = A				
TOTAL DEBTS = B				
NET WORTH A-B = net worth (assets minus total debts)				

Notes:

Budget

Income *(After tax)*

INCOME *(After tax)*	Budget Annual	Actual Annual	% of Income	Notes
Take Home Income	$	$	%	
Second Income				
Pension				
Allowance				
Commission				
Support				
Investment Income				
Dividends				
Rental Income				
Other				
TOTAL INCOME:	$	$		

Expenses

EXPENSES	Budget Annual	Actual Annual	% of Expense	Notes
HOUSING EXPENSES:	$	$	%	
Condo Strata fees				
Electrical Costs				
Gas for House				
Garbage/Sewer Costs				
Home Security				
House/Tenant Insurance				
Household Décor				
Household Furnishings				
Line of Credit				
Mortgage				
2nd Mortgage				
Other Heat Source Costs				
Property Taxes				
Rent				
Repairs				
Water Costs				
Other				
SUB TOTAL	$	$	%	

FOOD: GROCERY & DINING OUT	Budget	Actual	% of Expense	Notes
Dining Out	$	$	%	
Groceries				
Food Deliveries				
Pet Food				
Other				
SUB TOTAL	$	$	%	**Notes:** Food + groceries expenses cost 0-20% of total expenses

TRANSPORTATION	Budget	Actual	% of Expense	Notes
Fuel				
Parking				
Public Transit				
Roadside Assistance Program				
Taxi/Car Ride				
Vehicle Insurance				
Vehicle Loan/Lease Payment				
Vehicle Purchase Price				
Vehicle Rental				
Vehicle Repair/Maintenance				
Other				
SUB TOTAL			%	**Notes:** Transportation expenses cost 0-20% of total expenses

CLOTHING	Budget	Actual	% of Expense	Notes
Clothes	$	$	%	
Professional/Uniform				
Shoes				
Sports Clothes				
Other				
SUB TOTAL	$	$	%	**Notes:** Clothing expenses cost 3%-5% of total expenses

HEALTH EXPENSES	Budget	Actual	% of Expense	Notes
Deductibles				
Dental/Orthodontist				
Extended Health Care				
Glasses/Contacts				
Medical Premiums				
Optometry Eye Care				
Over the Counter				
Personal Disability insurance				
Personal Life Insurance				
Pet Insurance				
Prescriptions				
Specialists (Massage, Chiropractor, Physiotherapy				
Travel Medical Insurance				
Vet Bills				
Other				
SUB TOTAL			%	**Notes:** Medical Health expenses cost 0-5% of total expenses

PERSONAL EXPENSES	Budget	Actual	% of Expense	Notes
Alcohol	$	$	%	
Bank Fees Safety Deposit Box				
Books/Magazines				
Cable/Tv Costs				
Coffee/Snacks				
Donations				
Entertainment (movies, events, socials)				
Education				
Gifts Other				
Gifts Family				
Hair				
Hobbies Capital				
Hobbies Operating Costs				
HobbiesRepair/ Maintenance				
Laundry/Dry Cleaning				
Membership Fees				
Online Entertainment (movies, music)				
Personal Grooming (nails, waxing etc.)				
Phone Mobile				
Sports				
Tobacco/Vaping/Other				
Vacation				
Other				
SUB TOTAL	$	$	%	**Notes:** Personal expense cost 5%-20% of total expenses

CHILDREN EXPENSES	Budget	Actual	% of Expense	Notes
Allowance	$	$	%	
Babysitting				
Lessons				
School Fees				
School Supplies				
Other				
SUB TOTAL	$	$	%	**Notes:** Children expenses cost of total expenses

SAVINGS: Try to save 5% to 10% of your income every month	Budget	Actual	% of Expense	Notes
Savings into RESP (Registered Education Savings Plan)				
Savings into RRSP (Registered Retirement Savings Plan)				
Savings into TSFA (Tax Free Savings Account)				
Savings into Other Account				
SUB TOTAL			%	**Notes:** Saving expense cost 0-10% of total expenses

DEBTS REPAYMENTS	Budget	Actual	% of Expense	Notes
Child/Spousal Support				
Credit Card 1				
Credit Card 2				
Credit Card 3				
Income Tax Deductions				
Line of Credit				
Money Owed				
Other Debt Repayment				

Student Loans Repayment	$	$	%	
Other				
SUB TOTAL	$	$	%	
COST OF LIVING *Total Expenses*				
INCOME LESS EXPENSES				:

Monthly expenses at a glance	HOUSING	FOOD	TRANS-PORTATION	CLOTHES	HEALTH	PERSONAL	CHILDREN	SAVINGS
JAN								
FEB								
MARCH								
APRIL								
MAY								
JUNE								
JULY								
AUG								
SEPT								
OCT								
NOV								
DEC								
Monthly Totals	$	$	$	$	$	$	$	$

Notes:

Assets

Complete the following pages of asset details and attach copies or originals of your most current document of proof.

For instance, include most recent statements from banks, investments firms, Personal insurance, real estate title certificate, jewelry appraisals, personal property checklist, stock certificates, vehicle purchase/lease papers etc.

Assets

Name	City	Account No	Current Balance	Name on Account	Owner

LIFE INSURANCE					
Description of Policy	Premium	Death Benefit	Cash Value To Date	Owner	Beneficiary

REAL ESTATE	TYPE	Parcel Identity #	Purchase Price $	Current Value $	Owner

DEBTS OWED TO YOU	Type	$ Amount	Date Loaned	Date Collected	

PERSONAL ITEMS & EFFECTS					
Description	**Owner**	**Location**	**$ Value**	**Other**	
Vehicle and VIN					
OTHER ASSETS					
Description	**Owner**	**Location**	**Estimated Value**	**Other**	
Total $			$_____		

Notes:

Insurance

Complete the following pages of insurance details and attach copies or originals of your most current document of proof.

For instance, include most recent statements from Life Insurance Company, home insurance company, vehicle insurance documents, medical & dental insurance documents, travel insurance documents and other insurance papers.

Manage Me™

INSURANCE					
Insurance Type	Name	Account No	Current Cash Value	Coverage	Premium
PERSONAL:					
Annual cost of personal insurance:			$	$	$

INSURANCE					
Insurance Type	Name	Account No	Current Cash Value	Coverage	Premium
HOME:					
VEHICLE:					
MEDICAL:					
Travel Medical:					
Annual cost of personal insurance:			$	$	$

Notes:

Debts

Debts

Complete the following pages of debt details and attach copies or originals of your most current document of proof.

For instance, include most recent statements from bank loans, credit card statements, mortgage statements, and other liability statements.

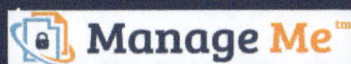

Manage Me™

DEBTS:	Bank Name	Account Number	Limit	Current Balance
Credit Cards				
Bank Loans				
Mortgage				
Car Loan				
Student Loan				
Line of Credit				
Other Debt				
Other Debt				
Total Debt				$

DEBTS:	Bank Name	Account Number	Limit	Current Balance
				$
Total Debt				$

Notes:

Estate Planning & Will

Complete the following estate planning questionnaire and include a copy of your most current Will.

The following estate planning questionnaire is a sample only and does not represent a legal Will.

Manage Me™

ESTATE PLANNING QUESTIONNAIRE

I.   YOUR PERSONAL INFORMATION

Name (full legal name and any other names by which you are known):

Address (please include alternate address if you split your residence among one or more than one place):

_____

Telephone: (home)_____   (office)_____

Mobile: _____   Fax: _____

Email: _____

Occupation: _____

Date of Birth (dd/mm/yy): _____

Place of Birth: _____

Marital Status: ☐ Single   ☐ Engaged   ☐ Married

                     ☐ Cohabiting   ☐ Separated   ☐ Divorced

Citizenship: _____

II. YOUR SPOUSE/COMMON LAW PARTNER (Please complete if applicable.) Name (full legal name and any other names by which he/she is also known):

Occupation: _____

Date of Birth (dd/mm/yy): _____

Place of Birth: _____

Citizenship: _____

Are you: ☐ Legally Married   ☐ Living in a Common Law Relationship

III. CHILDREN (Please complete if applicable)

Please list your children (and your spouses' children) including any adopted children.

Name	Date of Birth	Citizenship	Residence	Parents

Please indicate if any of your children have a disability, marital difficulties or are deceased.

IV.   NEXT OF KIN

Please provide the names and addresses of nearest living relatives (other than spouse and children referred to above) beginning with the first of the following list which apply:

- Lineal descendants (such as grandchildren, great-grandchildren, etc.) _____

- Parents: _____

- Siblings: _____

- Nieces and nephews: _____

- Grandparents: _____

- Aunts and uncles: _____

- Remoter relatives (such as cousins, etc.): _____

V.   OTHER DEPENDENTS

Is someone other than a spouse or child dependent upon you for financial assistance?

Yes ☐   No ☐

If yes, please provide name and relationship: _____

_____

VI.   MARRIAGE DETAILS (Please complete if applicable)

Date of Marriage: _____Place: _____

Country and Province/State of residence at time of marriage if different from place of marriage:

Did you sign a marriage agreement?	Yes ☐	No ☐
Have you signed a separation agreement?	Yes ☐	No ☐
Are there any on-going family law proceedings?	Yes ☐	No ☐
Have you been married previously?	Yes ☐	No ☐
Do you have maintenance obligation with respect to this former marriage?	Yes ☐	No ☐

Please provide us with a copy of any marriage, separation or property settlement agreements.

VII.   COMMON LAW RELATIONSHIPS

(both common law and same sex marriage-like relationship)

How long have you been cohabiting with your spouse/partner? _____

Do you have a cohabitation agreement?	Yes ☐	No ☐

If you have a cohabitation agreement, please provide us with a copy.

VIII.   OTHER LEGAL OBLIGATIONS

Are you currently serving as a guardian of a minor child?   Yes ☐   No ☐

Are you currently acting as committee of an incapacitated adult?   Yes ☐   No ☐

Are you currently acting as an executor or administrator of

an estate?   Yes ☐   No ☐

To your knowledge are you named as an executor under any

living person's will?   Yes ☐   No ☐

Are you acting as an attorney pursuant to an enduring power

of attorney?   Yes ☐   No ☐

If you answered 'yes' to any of the above please provide details.

_____

_____

_____

_____

IX.   ASSETS

Please indicate which of the following assets you own and include their location, the name or names in which they are held (i.e. your name, your spouse, joint names as joint tenants or tenants in common):

A. <u>REAL ESTATE</u>:

Home: _____

Street Address: _____

Legal Description (if known): _____

Mortgage: Yes ☐   No ☐

If yes, name of lender and approximate balance:_____

If yes, is mortgage life insured?   Yes ☐   No ☐

Date of Acquisition: _____

Acquisition Cost: _____

Name in which registered _____

Recreational:

Street Address: _____

Legal Description (if known): _____

Mortgage: Yes ☐   No ☐

If yes, name of lender and approximate balance: _____

If yes, is mortgage life insured?   Yes ☐   No ☐

Date of Acquisition: _____

Acquisition Cost: _____

Name in which registered: _____

Other:

Street Address: _____

Legal Description (if known): _____

Mortgage: Yes ☐   No ☐

If yes, name of lender and approximate balance: _____

If yes, is mortgage life insured?   Yes ☐   No ☐

Date of Acquisition _____

Acquisition Cost: _____

Name in which registered: _____

B. CASH:

Bank Accounts and Term Deposits. Please list (where accounts are in more than one name, please indicate nature of interest, i.e. joint tenants or purely signing for convenience).

Bank	Account Number	Approximate Current Balance	Name(s) on Account

Securities/Bonds/Shares (Public Companies). Please list (where held in brokerage account please indicate by *)

Issuer	Cash Value	Account No. (If applicable)	Name(s) on Account or Share Certificate	Original Cost	Restrictions

Interest in Private Company/Partnership/Proprietorship.

Description	Estimated Vaue	Name(s) of Owner(s)	Original Cost

If you own shares in a private company or have interest in a partnership, please provide a copy of any share agreements or buy/sell agreements or other documentation affecting your rights as an owner.

Pension.

Do you have an interest in any pension plans?   Yes ☐   No ☐

If so, who is the pension provider? _____

If so, who is the beneficiary on your death? _____

Are you the owner of any annuities?   Yes ☐   No ☐

If so, who is the annuity provided by? _____

If so, who are the named beneficiaries? _____

RRSP and RRIF (please list):

Description	Estimated Value	Owner	Beneficiary

Life Insurance (please list).

On your life:

Description	Death Benefit	Owner	Beneficiary(ies)

Of which you are the beneficiary

Description	Death Benefits	Owner	Beneficiary(ies)

Debts Owed to You (please list).

Description	Death Benefits	Owner	Current Balance

Personal Items and Effects (list any personal items of specific monetary or sentimental value).

Description	Owner	Estimated Value	Location

Do you have an interest in any estates or trusts?   Yes ☐   No ☐

If yes (please list):

Description	Estimated Value

Other Assets (please list).

Description	Death Benefits	Owner	Current Balance

If more space is required, please attach a separate page.

X.   LIABILITIES

Do you have any outstanding debts other than mortgage debts described in part VIII?   Yes ☐   No ☐

If yes:

Name of Lender	Account Owed	Debtor(s)	Life Insured

Have you guaranteed any loans or provided an indemnity for someone else?_____

If yes:

Name of Lender	Principal Debtor	Guarantor/ Indemnitor	Amount

XI.   OTHER ESTATE INFORMATION

Do you have an accountant and if so what is his or her name and address?

_____

Do you have a financial advisor and if so what is his or her name and address?

_____

XII.   WILL

Do you currently have a Will?   Yes ☐   No ☐

Please provide a copy of your current Will.

A.   Executors and Trustees

Who do you wish to appoint as your executor(s) and trustee(s) of your Will? Your executor(s) and trustee(s) will be the person or people who administer your estate pursuant to your will. Please indicate whether this person is to be an initial primary executor or whether they are to be an alternate.

Name	Address	Occupation	Relationship	Primary, Joint or Secondary

B. If you have minor children (under 19 years), who is to be his/her or their guardian(s) should you (and the other parent) die while they are minors? Please indicate whether this person is to be the primary guardian or an alternate.

Name	Address	Occupation	Relationship	Primary, Joint or Secondary

C. Do you have any specific instructions regarding your funeral that you wish included in your will?

Note: it is not necessary to include funeral instructions in your will.

_____

_____

_____

_____

_____

D.   Personal Effects

Are there any specific items you wish to give to someone in particular? If so, please list. If more space is needed please attach a separate list.

Name	Address	Relationship	Description

Who do you want to receive the remainder of your personal effects (i.e. clothing, jewellery, household goods, furniture, vehicles etc. not specifically gifted)?

_____

_____

_____

_____

E. Legacies

Do you wish to leave a cash gift to anyone (an individual or a charity)? Please attach a separate list if more space is needed.

Name	Address	Relationship	Amount

F. RRSP/RRIF (Complete if applicable)

Do you want to designate a beneficiary of any RRIF or RRSP?

Other than your estate?   Yes ☐   No ☐

If yes, who? _____

Do you intend that the tax burden associated with your RRIF/RRSP

will be borne by your estate even if the beneficiary is not your estate?   Yes ☐   No ☐

G. Pension (Complete if applicable)

Do you wish to make or change the beneficiary of your pension?   Yes ☐   No ☐

If so, to whom? _____

H.   Specific Gifts

Other than gifts of personal items or cash, do you wish to make any other specific gifts, such as a gift of a piece of land, shares, etc.? If yes, please list.   Yes ☐   No ☐

Name	Address	Relationship	Description of Gift

I.   Disposition of Residue (all assets not otherwise disposed of)

Please complete the appropriate sections below:

1.   Provision for spouse (please choose one):

(a)   Everything to spouse if survive me by 30 days   ☐

(b)   Everything held in trust for spouse during his or her lifetime to receive net income   ☐
            with power of trustees to encroach upon capital

(c)   Other (please specify):   ☐

_____

(d)   Nothing: ☐

Why: _____

2.   Provision for Children subject to any gifts to spouse above (please choose one):

(a)   Immediate equal division among children with children of deceased children   ☐
            taking deceased child's share

(b)   Equal division among children with deceased child's children taking deceased   ☐
            child's share with distribution to children at the following ages and in the
            following proportions:

            ___% at ___ years, ___% at ___ years, ___% at ___ years

(c)   Unequal division   ☐

Why: _____

(d)   None.   ☐

Why: _____

3. If the provisions made in paragraphs I. 1 and/or 2 fail or if they do not apply, who do you want to receive the residue of your estate (family, friends, charities)?

Name	Address	Relationship	Portion of Estate

If any of these beneficiaries are not living at the time the residue of your estate is distributed should their children take in their place?   Yes ☐   No ☐

J. Executor(s) and Trustee(s) Fees

Do you have any specific wishes concerning your executor(s) and trustee(s) fees?   Yes ☐   No ☐

Note: If your will is silent on this issue an executor and trustee may claim a <u>maximum</u> fee of 5% of the gross value of your estate plus an annual care and management fee of a <u>maximum</u> of 0.4% of the average value of your estate in addition to reimbursement for reasonable expenses.

If your executor(s) and trustee(s) is also a beneficiary under your will, do you wish them to receive a fee in addition to the gift they receive?   Yes ☐   No ☐

XIII.   MUTUAL WILLS (please complete where applicable)

If you and your spouse will sign Wills leaving everything to the other, is the survivor of you free to change his or her Will after the death of the first of you to die?

Yes ☐   No ☐

Please note that if your answer is "no" then you should discuss this issue with us further.

XIV.   INCAPACITY PLANNING

A.   Living Will

Do you have a Living Will?

Yes ☐   No ☐

If not, would you like to make a Living Will setting out your wishes as to the life supporting medical care you wish to receive if you are not able to give or refuse consent to medical care on your own behalf?

Yes ☐   No ☐

B.   Enduring Power of Attorney

Do you have an Enduring Power of Attorney?

Yes ☐   No ☐

If yes, please provide us with a copy of the document.

Do you wish to name an attorney to deal with your property and financial affairs?

Yes ☐   No ☐

If so, please provide:

Name	Address	Relationship	If more than one whether joint or separately

C.   Nomination of Committee

Have you made a Nomination of a Committee to be your legal guardian
in the event you are no longer capable of managing your   Yes ☐   No ☐
personal or financial affairs?

If you wish to make such a nomination, please provide the following information concerning your nominee:

Name	Address	Relationship	If more than one whether joint or separately

D.   Representation Agreement

Have you entered into a Representation Agreement in which you
name one or more persons as your representative(s) for   Yes ☐   No ☐
personal or financial matters?

If yes, please provide a copy.

Name	Address	Relationship	If more than one whether joint or separately

Notes:

Wallet

Complete the table of contents following and upload pictures of bank/credit cards, membership cards and other important cards in your wallet.

Card Name	Bank/Lender	Account No	If stolen/lost number to call

Card Name	Bank/Lender	Account No	If stolen/lost number to call

Personal Other

Include other documents such as resumes, personal certificates, educational diplomas & degrees, current warranties, subscriptions, rental contracts, etc.

What's in my Personal Other:

(List the documents that are included in this section)

le Reports, Warranties, Awards, Resume, Certificates, Contracts , Education

_____

_____

_____

_____

_____

_____

_____

_____

_____

_____

_____

_____

_____

_____

_____

_____

_____

_____

_____

_____

_____

_____

_____

PERSONAL ITEMS LOANED TO

Date:	Item:	To:	Returned:

Date:	Item:	To:	Returned:

Notes:

Manage Me, LMS Inc.

Life Management Systems

My Life Manager ©

My Health Manager ©

My Life Manager App launched 2021

www.manageme.ca

Email: info@manageme.ca

Published by Manage Me,

LMS (Life Management Systems), Inc.

ISBN 978-0-9869543-0-6

Manage Me™

www.ingramcontent.com/pod-product-compliance
Lightning Source LLC
Chambersburg PA
CBHW052343210326
41597CB00037B/6240